Our Community

Living in the Community

Pearson Australia
(a division of Pearson Australia Group Pty Ltd)
707 Collins Street, Melbourne, Victoria 3008
PO Box 23360, Melbourne, Victoria 8012
www.pearson.com.au

First published 2012 by Pearson Australia
2020 2019 2018 2017
10 9 8 7 6 5 4

Author: Jo Tayler
Publishers: Sarah Russell and Kirsty Hamilton
Project Editor: Rachel Davis
Editor: Cameron Macintosh
Designers: Anne Donald and Jeni Burton
Copyright & Pictures Editor: Sian Bradfield
Desktop Operator: Kate Hansen
Cover Designer: Glen McClay
Printed in Australia by the SOS Print + Media Group

National Library of Australia Cataloguing-in-Publication entry
Author: Tayler, Jo.
Title: Living in the community / Jo Tayler.
ISBN: 9781442559653 (pbk.)
Series: Our Community
Notes: Includes index
Target Audience: For primary school age.
Subjects: Communities--Juvenile literature.
Community life--Juvenile literature.
Dewey Number: 307

Pearson Australia Group Pty Ltd ABN 40 004 245 943

Acknowledgements
We would like to thank the following for permission to reproduce copyright material.
The following abbreviations are used in this list: t = top, b = bottom, l = left, r = right, c = centre.

Alamy Ltd: Bill Bachman, p. 9; Alex Segre, p. 17; Corbis Australia Pty Ltd: DeBrocke, p. 12; Howard Pyle, p. 16; David Moore Photography: David Moore, p. 6; Dreamstime: p. 11; Fairfax Photo Sales: Age Archives, p. 24; Phil Carrick, p. 23; Craig Golding, p. 25; Getty Images: FPG, p. 14; Westend61, p. 13; National Archives of Australia: D. Baglin (B941/1, 5984111), p. 8; Jack Band (A1200/18, 6816607), p. 4; (A8139/1, 8291704), p. 22; National Library of Australia: (nla.pic-an23697892-v), p. 10; News Limited Images (Newspix): Brett Costello, p. 5; The Courier-Mail Photo Archive, p. 20; Mark Smith, p. 15; Shutterstock: Ferenc Szelepcsenyi, p. 27; fmua, cover, pp. 19, 21; State Library of South Australia: Image courtesy of the State Library of South Australia and Arthur Studio (Mount Gambier, S. Aust.) SLSA: B 26176 – Harvey and John Temby, ca.1955, p. 26; State Library of Victoria: Mark Strizic, Pedestrians on Swanston Street, Melbourne 1955–1956 (H2008.11/1275), p.18; Tayler, Chris: p. 29; Thinkstock: p. 7.

Every effort has been made to trace and acknowledge copyright. However, if any infringement has occurred, the publishers tender their apologies and invite the copyright holders to contact them.

Some of the images used in *Our Community: Living in the Community* might have associations with deceased Indigenous Australians. Please be aware that these images may cause sadness or distress in Aboriginal or Torres Strait Islander communities.

Contents

Words that are printed in bold are explained in the Glossary on page 32.

What is a Community?

A community is a group of people with something in common. In the past, communities were made up of people close by, like your neighbours and the people at your school.

Today, the communities we live in are bigger. They still include your neighbours and school, but because of modern technology, we can easily stay in touch with friends and family interstate and overseas. Many of us belong to an online community too.

This book will show you how people lived in communities in the past and how people live in communities today.

Moving to Australia

Many people have moved from other countries to Australia. At first, most people came from England – some as convicts and some as settlers.

When gold was found, people came to Australia from all over the world, including China. After World War II (1939–1945), many people came from Europe.

People still come from all over the world to live in Australia, so our society has become very **multicultural**. We can have friends from all over the world. Many people still come from English-speaking countries, but others come from countries that are very poor or are at war.

City or Country?

In the past, there were more people living on farms in the country than there are today.

Life could be lonely on farms back then because it was harder to keep in touch with friends and relatives. Farmers might only go to town once a month, depending on how far away it was.

Our cities have grown, and they are now home to most people. It's easier to keep in touch now and cheap to fly and visit friends and family in other states. Kids living in really remote areas attend School of the Air, which is a school run over the internet.

School Community

At many schools in the past, there were as many as 40 or 50 students in each class.

Students had to learn many things by rote (repeating something over and over to remember it), such as the times tables. Many teachers were stricter than teachers are today.

Today, there are fewer students in each class in schools. In some classes, there may also be a teacher's aide helping. School is fun now. Students do many kinds of activities in class, such as role playing, keeping a kitchen garden and cooking.

Going to Work

When your grandparents were young, men went to work and most mothers stayed at home to look after the house and family.

Men were called the "breadwinners" because they earned the money to buy food and pay for the house. Working women were expected to leave their jobs when they got married.

Today, it's more common for both mums and dads to work. Women can do all the same jobs as men. People can choose to work part time or work from home. Some dads stay home to look after the house and family while the mum goes to work.

Getting Around

In the past, not as many families had a car and not many women could drive.

People would walk to the local shops to buy their groceries. Most kids walked or rode their bicycles to school. More people used public transport to get around.

Cars are cheaper these days, and many more people can afford them. Some families even have more than two cars and drive most places. Many people still use public transport, especially to go to busy places, such as the city centre and big sporting events.

Keeping in Touch

People used to write letters and use the telephone to keep in touch.

Long-distance phone calls were expensive, so you couldn't talk for too long. People spent time with neighbourhood friends at local sporting matches and church events. They saw friends and relatives who lived further away less often.

Today, we write letters and call people at home, but we also keep in touch with our friends electronically. We call on our mobile phones, send emails, make video calls and send texts and instant messages. Communication is more instant so our messages tend to be shorter.

Getting the Latest News

In the past, people read newspapers and listened to the radio to get the latest news.

To see moving pictures of news, people had to wait weeks for the film to arrive by boat from overseas. Television was available in Australia in 1956, but at first not many people had TVs.

Today, we see lots of information about what's happening in the world as it happens on television and the internet. We still read newspapers and listen to the radio, but now we can also do these things on computers or other electronic **devices**.

Leisure Time

Playing in the street and going to the football and the local cinema in the neighbourhood were popular leisure activities when your grandparents were young.

On summer holidays, people went camping or had picnics. They also stayed with relatives or friends in the country.

Today, we use modern technology to watch movies at home, play video games and play on the computer, so we are less active than previous **generations**. Many people enjoy going to shopping centres to hang out. More families can afford to take holidays interstate or overseas.

Sporting Events

Australians have always been sports mad! In the past, people would often go to watch their local football, cricket and other sporting teams play.

Back then, people also listened to sports on the radio – some matches were even **broadcast** from overseas.

Today, we are still sports mad! We play in and go to watch lots of local club matches and support our team when it plays nearby. A lot of sport is broadcast on television, and we can watch sport **live** from all over the world. Some TV channels *only* show sports.

Festivals and Celebrations

In the past, country shows were popular events each year.

People would enjoy seeing all the prize-winning animals, vegetables, crafts and cakes as well as rodeo competitions and sheepdog trials. When there was an important visitor in town, crowds would go to see the parade and welcome the visitor.

Today, we have lots of festivals celebrating different cultures and nationalities. We can experience all sorts of music, dance and food. We celebrate sporting grand finals with parades and awards for the best players. There is usually an Aboriginal 'welcome to country' at the start of ceremonies.

Doing the Shopping

People used to walk to the local general store to buy most of their food and other things needed for the house.

In the past, some items, such as milk, were home delivered. The clip-clop of horses' hooves would tell you when the milkman was near.

Today, there are large shopping centres with hundreds of shops under the one roof. You can go there to shop, eat and see a movie. They have large car parks around them because most people drive there. You can also buy almost anything you want online.

Sophia and June

Sophia and her grandma, June, tell us about life in their community.

Sophia

"My family lives in the city. My great-grandparents live in the country, and we visit them at Christmas.

Mum and Dad both work four days a week, and the other days they stay home.

Dad likes to read magazines on his iPad. Mum checks the news on TV or the internet. When I'm not busy, I play in my room, read books and draw.

There are 22 kids in my class at school. Sometimes we drive to school but usually I go on the scooter. Mum and Dad have two cars."

June

"I grew up in a suburb of Melbourne. Mum stayed at home and Dad worked six days a week. Dad had a car for his work as a real estate agent.

"I took the train to school and walked or took a bus to the local football games. I rode my bicycle around the local area too, and played with other kids in the street.

We had the newspaper delivered and Dad would read it at the breakfast table. We also listened to the radio a lot. There was no television back then."

Comparison Table

	In the Past
Australia's Population	most people came from England
Where People Live	many people lived in cities, some lived in the country
School	more students per classroom, more formal
Going to Work	fathers worked, most mothers stayed at home
Getting Around	not many people had cars, people walked and took public transport
Keeping in Touch	letters, telephone, **telegrams**
News and Current Affairs	newspapers and radio
Leisure Time	playing and watching sport, cinema, church, picnics
Sports	playing and watching, listening to radio **broadcasts**
Festivals and Celebrations	country shows, parades
Shopping	local grocers, butchers and general store; walk to the shops; milkman delivered milk

	Today
	people come from all over the world
	most people live in cities, fewer live in the country
	smaller classes, more variety in lessons
	fathers and mothers work, there are more flexible work conditions
	most people drive cars, many people use public transport
	mobile phones, email, video calls, instant messaging
	television, internet, newspapers and radio
	playing and watching sport, watching television, playing video games, shopping
	playing and watching, watching sport on TV and the internet
	local council and **multicultural** festivals, music festivals
	shopping at supermarkets and shopping centres; shopping online

Glossary

broadcast to send messages by radio or television

convict a criminal serving a prison sentence

devices inventions, equipment

generation all the people born around the same time

live something that is being watched by broadcast as it happens

multicultural with many cultures or people from many countries in the world

settler a person or family moving to live in a different country

telegram an urgent short message on paper delivered by hand

Index